Memorable
Senior MOMENTS

*God bless you!
Mama Mary,
loves you!*

Fr. Jerry

FR. JERRY M. ORBOS, SVD

The **Society of the Divine Word (SVD)** is an international missionary congregation of priests and brothers serving in more than fifty countries all over the world. Through the **Logos Publications,** the SVD in the Philippines aims to foster the apostolate of the printed word in the biblical, theological, catechetical and pastoral fields in order to promote justice, peace and human development. The opinions of the author do not necessarily reflect those of the SVD community.

Bible passages were taken from The New American Standard Bible (NASB), The New Revised Standard Version of the Bible (NRSV), and The New King James Version (NKJV).

With approval from **Fr. Nielo Cantilado, SVD**
Provincial Superior, SVD Central Province, Philippines.

First Printing 2013
Copyright 2013 **Society of the Divine Word**
Published by **Logos Publications, Inc.**
All rights reserved

Printed by **Milcar Enterprises**
Quezon City, Philippines

ISBN 978-971-510-251-3

EDICATION

I lovingly dedicate this book to
my 92-year-old mother

Concepcion Muñoz-Orbos

who has shown me

what it is like

to

grow old gracefully

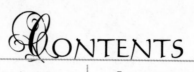ONTENTS

INTRODUCTION

I am 60 years old this October 1, 2013. In celebration of my senior citizenship, I came up with this book, "Memorable Senior Moments," to appreciate people who have braved the noonday sun, and are now journeying toward the sunset years of their lives.

This book is a collection of funny anecdotes, touching and meaningful stories, and reflections about growing old. Let us delight in the humor that the elderly bring to us, treasure the values and lessons they teach us, and be truly edified and inspired by their lives.

"Lord, grant me the grace to live the rest of my life, the best of my life!" This is our prayer. This is our hope. Yes, the best is yet to come!

God bless you.
Mama Mary loves you!

One with you,

Fr. Jerry

Korean birthday

I spent four years (1984-1988) in Korea as a missionary. One of the first things I learned there was that Koreans celebrate only two birthdays in their lifetime with a bang: their first *("Tol")* and their sixtieth birthday *("Hwan-gap")*.

Why? In Korea where infant mortality before was high, it was a big reason to celebrate a child's first birthday. And when one reaches 60 years of age, the Koreans already equate it to a full life. So, any year after 60 was considered as a 'bonus' already.

Every birthday is a thanksgiving day to God who gave us life, and to our parents who loved us and took care of us.

Every birthday, too, is like a kilometer sign post along the way to remind us how far we have gone down the road of life... and how near we are to our final destination! ❊

A moment with the *Lord*
Thank You, Lord, I was born in this world. Thank You, Lord, I'm still alive.
Help me to live a life that is full, beautiful and meaningful. Amen.

A moment with the *Word*
"Truly You have formed my inmost being; You knit me in
my mother's womb."   Psalm 139:13

Mea culpa!

*D*riving one morning, I was stopped by a traffic enforcer. As he approached my car, I said to myself that I won't let this guy get anything from me as I was sure that I didn't commit any traffic violation.

I opened my car window, and before he could say anything, I asked him what my offense was without hiding my anger and irritation. Then he told me, "Sir, you must have forgotten this on the roof of your car," as he handed to me my precious appointment notebook!

I was so embarrassed with my "senior moment," but more so embarrassed for misjudging his character and intentions.

Mea culpa! Mea culpa! Mea maxima culpa! ✺

A moment with the *Lord*
Lord, as I grow older, I may become forgetful, but please help me not to become angry nor resentful. Amen.

A moment with the *Word*
"But the Spirit produces love, joy, peace, patience, kindness, goodness, faithfulness, humility, and self-control." Galatians 5:22

Careful!

Somewhere in Spain, during a recent pilgrimage, I wanted to ask the name of a courteous sales lady. At that moment, I could not recall the Spanish word for "name"(*nombre*). I only remembered the Latin word for it, so I asked her, "*Nomen?*" I was astounded when, with a smile, she said, "No, I have no men, but I plan to have one in the future!" ❋

A moment with the *Lord*
Lord, help me not to miss the beauty and surprises of life with all its twists and turns. Amen.

A moment with the *Word*
"You have put gladness in my heart." Psalm 4:7

Remembering Papa

June 23, 1987 was a very sad day in my life.

It was the day that my father died. I miss my father. In fact, the pain is never really gone. I look forward to seeing him and embracing him again in heaven. While there is pain, I have no regrets whenever I think of my late father.

Why? Because I really loved him as much as I could while he was still alive. I really did my best for him. ✳

A moment with the *Lord*

Lord, help me to live with much love so that I won't have much regrets in life. Amen.

A moment with the *Word*

"I have loved you with an everlasting love, so I continue to show you my constant love." Jeremiah 31:3

Reminders from God

ecently, I saw an elderly man in a restaurant who looked like our Papa. I just sat there looking at the man, remembering Papa — praying for him, and asking him to pray for us all. For me, it was a moment of grace, a beautiful reminder from God that our loved ones are never really gone.

And guess what? That evening, an old friend and co-worker of Papa called me from out of the blue to tell me that he was sending some fruits for me and for our missionaries. Yes, there are many things we cannot explain or understand in this life. With faith we know and believe that God is so present, so alive, and that our loved ones who have gone ahead of us, are never gone. ✺

A moment with the Lord
Lord, thank You for the memories and for the reminders that we are loved. Amen.

A moment with the Word
"As the Father loved me, I also have loved you; abide in My love." John 15:9

Then and now

$\int$omewhere in Makati, a shabby old man knocked on my car window and asked for some money. Seeing his condition, I gave him some cash, for which he thanked me profusely, and even asked for my name. When he heard my name, he asked me how I was related to Guillermo Orbos. Upon learning that he was my father, tears welled in his eyes, as he told me that it was Papa who helped him get a job some 30 years ago.

This happened on June 22, the eve of my Papa's death anniversary.

Yes, good deeds are remembered.

A good person is never gone. ❈

A moment with the *Lord*
Lord, while I live, let me sow seeds of kindness that people will long remember and never forget. Amen.

A moment with the *Word*
"Do not grow weary in doing good."   2 Thessalonians 3:13

(Ms. Julie Andrews, on her 70th birthday, sang this for the benefit of the American Association for Retired Persons.)

My favorite things

Botox and nose drops and needles for knitting,
Walkers and handrails and new dental fittings,
Bundles of magazines tied up in string,
These are a few of my favorite things.

Cadillacs and cataracts, hearing aids and glasses,
Polident and Fixodent and false teeth in glasses,
Pacemakers, golf carts and porches with swings,
These are a few of my favorite things.

When the pipes leak, when the bones creak,
When the knees go bad,
I simply remember my favorite things,
And then I don't feel so bad.

Hot tea and crumpets and corn pads for bunions,
No spicy hot food or food cooked with onions,
Bathrobes and heating pads and hot meals they bring,
These are a few of my favorite things.

Back pain, confused brains and no need for sinnin',
Thin bones and fractures and hair that is thinnin',
And we won't mention our short shrunken frames,
When we remember our favorite things.

When the joints ache, when the hips break,
When the eyes grow dim,
Then I remember the great life I've had,
And then I don't feel so bad.

A moment with the Lord

*Lord, instead of being burdened, teach me to sing my blues away
because You love me. Amen.*

A moment with the Word

*"Give thanks to the God of heaven, for his steadfast love
endures forever."*   Psalm 136:26

Moments of grace

I praise and thank God for blessing Mama with 92 years of life. Aside from periodic bouts with arthritis, she is healthy, alert, and ambulatory. I thank God for beautiful and meaningful moments spent with her when we go together down memory lane, and I listen to her stories, lessons, hopes, and dreams. I like it most when she would spontaneously burst into a smile or laughter when she remembers a happy incident or a person she recalls with fondness.

All her life, she has shown a deep love for others and a deep faith in God. ✳

A moment with the *Lord*
Lord, thank You for moments of grace with our loved ones.
Amen.

A moment with the *Word*
"I have cared for you from the time you were born. I am your God and will take care of you until you are old and your hair is gray. I made you and will care for you." Isaiah 46:3

Visiting Mama

No matter how busy I am, I always try to drop by the house and visit Mama. How happy and appreciative she is as soon as she sees me, smiling sweetly, and with arms outstretched to welcome me. I feel really home when I am with her -- no pressures, no agenda, no obligations. In every visit, we exchange stories and how-have-you-beens. Mama always has a simple meal prepared for me, or shares with me a special food she had set aside. This trait she got from her own mother, our *Bai Tinay*. Short or long, every visit is a delight for both of us, and ends with a prayer. Oftentimes, Mama has something for me to bring along – a good book she had read, a box of chocolates she had kept, or a little cash she had saved. When it is time to say goodbye, Mama would walk me to the door and lingers there. She would wave at me with a loving smile, waiting for the time I'll visit her again or just drop by. ✻

A moment with the *Lord*
Lord, remind me that time spent with loved ones is always precious. Amen.

A moment with the *Word*
"In Your presence is fullness of joy." Psalm 16:11

Slippers for Mama

One time when I came home from a pilgrimage, I gifted my Mama with a pair of soft room slippers. As I was putting them on her feet, I could not hold back my tears, remembering how she bought shoes or slippers for me and put them on me when I was a child. I was just overwhelmed with gratitude for having been given the chance to do the same for her in her old age. Now she has no money to buy me a pair of slippers. But she has so much love and gratitude for all who care for her. ✲

A moment with the *Lord*
Lord, thank You for the privilege of being able to let our loved ones feel how much we love them. Amen.

A moment with the *Word*
"Behold your Mother."   John 19:27

The one who kneels

*M*ama rarely asks for anything from her children. One evening though, she whispered to me that she has a small request. When I asked her what it was, she told me to get her a kneeler.

Why? She attends EWTN TV Mass every day and even now, at 92, she wants to kneel down during the Consecration and during Holy Communion.

Such simple, childlike, and humble love and devotion for the Eucharist. 🌟

A moment with the *Lord*
Lord, help me to love and live the Eucharist in my life. Amen.

A moment with the *Word*
"Truly, truly, I say to you, whoever believes has eternal life..."
John 6:47

Loving back

One evening, I found myself in tears as I was spoon-feeding my Mama. Perhaps because she was ill and weak, and she obeyed everything I told her to do like a little child.

I remembered how she had lovingly taken care of me as her little child, especially when I was sick.

Praise God for any opportunity or chance given to us to love back those who love us. ✺

A moment with the Lord
Lord, let me not miss or postpone any chance of loving back. Amen.

A moment with the Word
"I love you." John 15:9

'I will wait for you'

My grandmother, the mother of Mama, was a very prayerful and Marian person. Every time we'd visit her in San Carlos, Pangasinan, she would ask me, "Jerry, how many more years before you become a priest?" I would answer, "15 more years, 12 more years, 5 more years and so on. Every time I'd tell her how many more years before my ordination, she would always say with a smile, "I'll wait for you…"

And she did! My grandmother died at the age of 96 on October 25, 1980, the very same day I was ordained a priest at the Divine Word Seminary, Tagaytay. I was ordained about 10:00 in the morning, and *Bai Tinay*, my grandmother, died about 3:00 in the afternoon. My first Mass was a funeral Mass for a woman who prayed for me, encouraged me, and waited for me to become a priest. ✳

A moment with the *Lord*
Lord, through the years, You have manifested Your concrete signs and wonders in my life. You are a God who is real, and Your presence in my life is real. Amen.

A moment with the *Word*
"I remember you in my prayers night and day." 2 Timothy 1:3

Love knows

$\mathcal{I}$t was a brief encounter in the elevator but it had such a lasting effect on me.

At the Rimonin Hotel in the Holy Land, I boarded the elevator together with a woman who was lovingly leading her elderly mother. Not wanting to let an opportunity to pass, I told the mother how lucky she was to have a loving daughter by her side, and I complimented the daughter for her filial love.

I also took the occasion to tell them a little about Mama — her joys and wishes. When we parted, I congratulated the mother again for having such a good daughter. Then she told me, "From the way you speak, you too must be a good son."

I smiled, and I said to myself, "Yes, God knows I am… God knows I try." ✺

A moment with the Lord
Lord, remind me that if my loving is true and sincere,
it shows even without my saying it. Amen.

A moment with the Word
"Love is patient, love is kind. It does not envy,
it does not boast, it is not proud."   *I Corinthians 13:4*

Priestly 'senior moment'

*I*t was his golden jubilee and the septuagenarian was the main presider during the Mass. Everything went well until he came to the Consecration part. Saying "This is my body which will be given up for you," he raised the host solemnly, put down the host, bowed his head, and proceeded to consume the host before any of the priest concelebrants could stop him!

Next, he said: "When supper was ended, he took the cup… he took the cup… where is the cup?" and one of the concelebrants quickly handed him the chalice. That went well. But when Communion time came, before he said, "This is the Lamb of God who takes away the sin of the world…" he paused and asked, "Where is the bread?" and all of the concelebrants chorused, "You already ate it, Father!" ✺

A moment with the *Lord*
Lord, even if we forget You, You will never forget us. Amen.

A moment with the *Word*
"It is the Lord who goes before you. He will be with you; He will not leave you or forsake you."   Deuteronomy 31:8

'Something wrong?'

This story was told by a priest who visited Fr. Alphonse Mildner, SVD, in our retirement house at Christ the King Seminary. When Father Alphonse, who was a bit hard of hearing, asked him who he was, the priest told him: "I'm Bob, Father, your former novice," tapping his own chest. The second time Father Mildner asked who he was, the priest said the same thing, tapping his chest again. Then Father Mildner blurted out: "Something wrong with your chest?" ✺

A moment with the Lord
Lord, always remind me that actions speak louder than words. Amen.

A moment with the Word
"My child, hold on to your wisdom and insight. Never let them get away from you."   Proverbs 3:21

'Positive!'

$\mathcal{I}$ was passing by Villa Cristo Rey, our retirement house at Christ the King Seminary, when octogenarian Fr. Val Darunday, SVD, called me, shouting "Positive! Jerry. Positive!" As I approached him, he said with a big smile: "I am positive for prostate cancer!"

Wow! He said it so naturally and so matter-of-factly.

For me, Father Val personifies a disciple who has taken up his cross daily, and followed his Master joyfully and trustingly all these years! *

A moment with the $\mathscr{L}$ord
Lord, help me to trust You fully, and joyfully. Amen.

A moment with the $\mathscr{W}$ord
"Whoever wishes to be my follower must deny his very self, take up his cross each day, and follow my steps." Luke 9:23

Long winding homily

Fr. JB Barbieto, SVD

I was chaplain of the Pink Sisters in Baguio City for some time. One Saturday evening I got a telephone call from a lady who said, "I am Mrs. Co. I attended your Mass last Sunday and I was disappointed with your long homily."

I laughed and said, "Mrs. Co, last Sunday I was in Manila. Sorry, I don't have the gift of bilocation. The priest who took my place in the Mass was Father P. Now Mrs. Co, please tell me about the homily of Father P."

She said, "Father JB, the homily took about half an hour because the priest was repeating and repeating the same thing he was saying. My two kids fell asleep and the person next to me kept looking at her watch. He was like a classroom teacher, saying 'number 1, number 2, number 3, etc.' He was like a pilot flying his plane around and does not know where and how to land. OK, Father JB, I thought you were the homilist because the priest was also bald like you."

I thanked Mrs. Co and told her, "I learned something for my ministry from you. Now I know what I should not do. God bless you! Goodnight!" ✺

A moment with the Lord
Lord, remind me that I am never too old to learn. Amen.

A moment with the Word
"For wisdom will come into your heart, and knowledge will be pleasant to your soul; discretion will watch over you..."   Proverbs 2:10-11

Best time to pray

a boy asked an old man: "Sir, when is the best time to pray?"

The old man replied: "My son, the best day to pray is the day before you die."

Asked the boy: "But how can I possibly know the day when I will die?"

The old man said: "Precisely! We do not know when we will die. That's why we need to pray every single day of our life."

Remember, life is short. Let's make every day the best day of our life. ❀

A moment with the *Lord*
Lord, life is short. Help me not to postpone my conversion, and my loving. Amen.

A moment with the *Word*
"Show me O Lord, my life's end and the number of my days; let me know how fleeting is my life." Psalm 39:4

Senility Prayer

(written on a bookmark)

"*G*rant me the senility to forget the people I never liked,
the good fortune to run into the people I do like,
and the eyesight to tell the difference."

A moment with the *Lord*
Lord, help me to always see the bright, the light,
and the right side of life. Amen.

A moment with the *Word*
"*Accept one another, then, for the glory of God, as Christ has*
accepted you."   Romans 15:7

Stay with me, Lord

Prayer of Padre Pio

Stay with me, Lord, for it is necessary to have You present so that I do not forget You. You know how easily I abandon You.

Stay with me, Lord, because I am weak and I need Your strength, that I may not fall so often.

Stay with me, Lord, for You are my life, and without You, I am without fervor.

Stay with me, Lord, for You are my light, and without You, I am in darkness.

Stay with me, Lord, to show me Your will.

Stay with me, Lord, so that I hear Your voice and follow You.

Stay with me, Lord, for I desire to love You very much, and always be in Your company.

Stay with me, Lord, if You wish me to be faithful to You.

Stay with me, Lord, for as poor as my soul is, I wish it to be a place of consolation for You, a nest of Love.

Stay with me, Jesus, for it is getting late and the day is coming to a close, and life passes, death, judgment, eternity approaches. It is necessary to renew my strength, so that I will not stop along the way and for that, I need You. I fear the darkness, the temptations, the dryness, the cross, the sorrows.

Let me recognize You as Your disciples did at the breaking of bread, so that the Eucharistic Communion be the light which disperses the darkness, the force which sustains me, the unique joy of my heart.

Stay with me, Lord, because at the hour of my death, I want to remain united to You, if not by Communion, at least by grace and love.

Stay with me, Jesus, I do not ask for divine consolation, because I do not merit it, but, the gift of Your Presence, oh yes, I ask this of You!

Stay with me, Lord, for it is You alone I look for. Your love, Your grace, Your will, Your heart, Your spirit, because I love You and ask no other reward but to love You more and more."

Hear ye! Hear ye!

The story is told about three senior citizens, who were a bit hard of hearing, having a conversation in a porch.

The first one said, "Today is windy, isn't it?"

The second one said, "It's Thursday!"

And the third one said, "Me too, I'm thirsty. Let's drink!" ✻

A moment with the *Lord*

Lord, grant me the grace to hear, and beyond that, to listen. Amen.

A moment with the *Word*

"Oh, that today you would hear His voice, harden not your heart."
Hebrews 3:7-8

Trials and tribulations

The story is told about three elderly ladies who were discussing the trials and tribulations of getting older.

One said, "Sometimes I catch myself with a jar of mayonnaise in my hand while standing in front of the refrigerator, and I can't remember whether I need to put it away or start making a sandwich."

The second lady chimed in, "Yes, sometimes I find myself on the landing of the stairs and I can't remember whether I was on my way up, or on my way down."

The third one responded, "Well, ladies, I'm glad I don't have that problem, knock on wood," as she tapped her knuckles on the table and then said, "That must be the door, I'll get it!" ☀

A moment with the Lord
Lord, help me not to forget Your love and presence, especially in my senior years. Amen.

A moment with the Word
"My presence will go with you, and I will give you rest."
Exodus 33:14

Freeway

*D*id you hear about a senior citizen, who, driving on the freeway, received a frantic call from his wife, saying: "Honey, be careful! I just heard on the news that there's a car going the wrong way on the freeway."

"Gosh," he said, "it's not just one car. There are hundreds of them!" ✳

A moment with the *Lord*
Lord, remind me that there is no such thing as freeway,
all the way. Amen.

A moment with the *Word*
"Show me the path where I should walk, O Lord; point out the right
road for me to follow…" Psalm 25

'Parkinson's or Alzheimer's?'

*T*he story is told about an old man who was asked: "At your age, sir, what would you prefer, Parkinson's or Alzheimer's?"

He said: "I'd rather have Parkinson's. Better to spill half of my wine than to forget where I kept the bottle!" ✸

A moment with the *Lord*
Lord, help me to see and keep on seeing my blessings,
not what is missing! Amen.

A moment with the *Word*
"Be thankful in all circumstances. This is what God wants from you in
your life in union with Christ Jesus."   I Thessalonians 5:18

Never forget
Dik Trofeo

*I*t was the day off of the driver, and my 64-year- old brother-in-law volunteered to drive the car and bring his wife to the grocery store, which he did quite well. He even pushed the grocery cart while they were shopping, and he did well too. When they were done, he told his wife to wait at the entrance while he went to the parking lot to get the car. On that one, he didn't do quite well.

Why? He drove straight home, and only when the gate was opened did he realize that his wife was not with him! He went back to the grocery store in a huff, and found his wife, fuming mad. She gave him the silent treatment on their way home. The cold war had begun. ✻

A moment with the *Lord*
Lord, help me to remember. Help me not to never forget what and who is really important in my life. Amen.

A moment with the *Word*
"Let not steadfast love and faithfulness forsake you; write them on the tablet of your heart." Proverbs 3:3

What remains

*T*he story is told about two elderly ladies who were discussing the upcoming dance party at the country club.

"We're supposed to wear something that matches our husband's hair, so I'm wearing black," said Mrs. Smith.

"Oh my," said Mrs. Jones, "I'd better not go." ✺

A moment with the *Lord*
Lord, remind me that clothes may fade, and hairlines may recede, but love remains. Amen.

A moment with the *Word*
"I know that Your goodness and love will be with me all my life; and Your house will be my home as long as I live."   Psalm 23:6

True love waits

The story is told about a waitress who noticed something unusual as she served an elderly couple. The man began to eat his meal while his wife stared patiently out the window.

"Is there something wrong with your food?" the waitress asked the lady.

"No, the food looks great," she replied.

"Aren't you afraid your food will get cold if you wait much longer to eat?" the waitress queried further.

"Oh," the lady replied, "that's alright."

"Well, aren't you hungry?" the waitress finally asked.

"I sure am," the lady replied. "I'm just waiting until my husband gets through with the teeth." ✻

A moment with the *Lord*
Lord, remind me that true love involves sacrifice, patience, and lots of waiting. Amen.

A moment with the *Word*
"Love is patient and kind."   I Corinthians 13:4

Shoplifting

*T*he story is told about an old woman who was arrested for shoplifting at a grocery store. When she appeared before the judge, the judge asked what she had taken. The lady replied, "A can of peaches."

The judge then asked why she had done it. She replied, "I was hungry and forgot to bring any cash to the store."

The judge asked how many peaches were in the can. She replied, "Nine."

The judge said, "Well then, I'm going to give you nine days in jail—one day for each peach."

As the judge was about to drop his gavel, the lady's husband raised his hand. The judge asked, "Yes, what do you have to add?" The husband replied, "Your honor, she also stole a can of peas!" ✳

A moment with the Lord
*Lord, in the midst of prisons and limitations,
help me to see the humor in any life situation. Amen.*

A moment with the Word
"You have put gladness in my heart." Psalm 4:7

One more smile

*I*n the renewal of vows on their 60th wedding anniversary, Aurelio Bautista said to his wife, "I have loved you *Auring* all these years." To which Aurora simply replied, "I loved you twice as much all these years!"

How do relationships last? On a 50/50 basis? No, that's just about on the survival mode. More rightly, lasting relationships happen because one or the other, or both, went the extra mile and gave one more smile. ✳

A moment with the *Lord*
Lord, help me to go out of my way – to keep going the extra mile, and keep giving the extra smile. Amen.

A moment with the *Word*
"Love always protects, always trusts, always hopes, always perseveres."   *1 Corinthians 13:4-8*

The hairbrush
Venchie Paminiano

*S*ince my mother died, my father never remarried. He remained a widower for 20 years now. He really loved my mother so much that he decided to remain single for the rest of his life, just spending his senior years with his children and grandchildren.

Let me narrate a very touching, but funny story about my father and my son, Lance. During my father's Christmas vacation in our home, my son saw in our bathroom a hairbrush that was very old and quite stinky. When he asked me who owns the hairbrush, I told him it's his *Lolo's,* and the hairbrush was given by my mom. He immediately went to my father's room, bringing the hairbrush with him, and asked his *Lolo* the story behind it. While listening to their conversation, to my surprise, the hairbrush that my father is still using up to now was the very first anniversary gift that my mother gave him — 40 years ago!

A simple gift, yet very precious to my father. For me, it is a perfect example of the undying love of my father for my mother. My father cherished every single moment with my mother while she was still alive, with the presence of a very simple, yet meaningful gift: a hairbrush. ❋

A moment with the *L*ord
Lord, help me to leave behind not only my footprints but also my heartprints in this life. Amen.

A moment with the *W*ord
"Love never ends."　　　I Corinthians 13:8

eautiful story passed on to me by Leopoldo Veroy.)

The letter in the wallet
author unknown

I stumbled on a wallet someone had lost on the street. It contained a letter which I opened, hoping to find some clue. Then I saw the date — 1924!

It was written in a beautiful feminine handwriting on powder blue stationery with a little flower on the left-hand corner. It was a "Dear John" letter that told the recipient, Michael, that the writer could not see him anymore. It was signed, Hannah.

I made some calls and tracked down the address on the envelope. I found out that Hannah was staying in a nursing home. Hannah was a silver-haired woman with a warm smile. I told her about the wallet and showed her the letter. She took a deep breath and said, "Young man, this letter was the last contact I ever had with Michael."

She looked away for a moment deep in thought and then said softly, "I loved him very much, but I was only sixteen that time and my mother felt I was too young. Oh, he was so handsome. "Yes," she continued. "Michael Goldstein was a wonderful person. If you could find him, tell him I think of him often. And… " she hesitated for a moment, almost biting her lip, "tell him I still love him," she said smiling as tears began to well up in her eyes. "I never did marry. I guess no one ever matched up to Michael."

After saying goodbye to Hannah, I went outside and took out the brown leather wallet. When the guard saw it, he said "Hey, wait a minute! That's Mr. Goldstein's wallet. I'd know it anywhere with that bright red lacing. "

I asked him who Mr. Goldstein is. "He's one of the old timers on the 8th floor." I quickly ran back and went to the 8th floor where I was greeted by a nurse. We went to the reading room and saw a man reading a book. The nurse went over to him and asked if he had lost his wallet. Mr. Goldstein looked up with surprise, put his hand in his back pocket and said, "Oh, it is missing!"

I handed Mr. Goldstein the wallet and told him that I read the letter. "I think I know where Hannah is." "Hannah? You know where she is? How is she? Is she still as pretty as she was? Please, please tell me," he begged. "She's fine... just as pretty as when you knew her."

The old man smiled and asked, "Could you tell me where she is?" He grabbed my hand and said, "You know Mister, I was so in love with that girl that when that letter came, my life ended. I never married. I guess I've always loved her."

I asked Mr. Goldstein to come with me down to the third floor. We made our way to the day room where Hannah was sitting alone, watching television. "Hannah," the nurse said softly, pointing to Michael, who was standing in the doorway. "Do you know this man?" She adjusted her glasses, looked for a moment but didn't say a word. Michael said softly, "Hannah, it's Michael. Do you remember me?" She gasped, "Michael, I don't believe it! Michael! It's you! My Michael!" He walked slowly towards her and they embraced.

The nurse and I left with tears streaming down our faces. "See," I said. "See how the good Lord works! If it's meant to be, it will be."

After three weeks, I got a call. Michael and Hannah are going to tie the knot! I stood as Michael's best man. It was a beautiful wedding. If you ever wanted to see a 76-year-old bride and a 79-year-old groom acting like teenagers, you had to see this couple. ✻

A moment with the 𝓛ord
Lord, You really do make all things beautiful in Your time.
Help me to just trust in You. Amen.

A moment with the 𝓦ord
"He had made everything beautiful in His time."   *Ecclesiastes 3:11*

Two things to ask

An old fellow fell in love with a lady. He got down on his knees and told her there were two things he would like to ask her. She said, "OK."

He asked: "Will you marry me?"

She replied: "Yes."

When she asked him what his second question was, he replied: "Will you help me up?" ✻

'Sweetheart'

*T*here is a story about a little boy who told his grandfather: "Grandpa, I'm so inspired that up to now, you still call grandma 'sweetheart.'" The grandfather whispered to the grandson: "Don't tell this to grandma, OK? You see, I have forgotten her name!" ✳

A moment with the ℒord
Lord, thank You for always remembering my name. Amen.

A moment with the 𝒲ord
"I will never forget you." Isaiah 49:15

Not alone

Do you miss a loved one who had gone ahead? Below is a poem I read somewhere titled "Alone, But Not Alone."

Alone yet never quite alone.
I have an empty chair
But sometimes in the silence,
I imagine you are there.
The good companion of the past,
no longer here with me;
And yet in some mysterious ways,
you keep me company.
Thought or spirit?
Does it matter?
Words are meaningless.
I only know that in my times
of greatest loneliness,
I felt that you are somewhere near
though nothing's seen or said,
the bitter moment passes and
my heart is comforted.
I receive the strength I need,
am rescued from despair;
Maybe that's the way God works -
the answer to a prayer.
Though the pain is never lost
and the future is unknown,
I face the years that lie ahead,
alone, yet not alone...

A moment with the Lord

Lord, because of You and the resurrection, I am never alone.
I will never be alone. Amen.

A moment with the Word

"I am the resurrection and the life. Whoever believes in me,
though he die; yet shall he live."   John 11:25

Lovers in Paris
Chito Bello

*I*n one of our stops in Paris, we were given an extra hour to spend freely. The group agreed to see the sights and meet in a spot after an hour so we can be on time for our next destination. As Flor and I hopped from one shop after another, we got so enthralled that we forgot we had a curfew!

We even strolled leisurely, holding hands! Cheesy as it may seem, I imagined we were like the lovers in Paris. See, I can be romantic too! Who wouldn't be in a romantic place like that? Luckily, our tour guide insisted on making the bus go around the area several times because two passengers were missing! Oh, how embarrassing! But come to think of it, it was a very special one hour of "senior moment" with my wife whom I dated in Paris!

Looking back now, it is indeed true that if you don't learn to laugh at embarrassing moments, you won't have anything to laugh at when you are old. ✳

A moment with the *Lord*
*Lord, thank You for being
an understanding and loving God. Amen.*

A moment with the *Word*
*"Because you are precious to me and honored,
I love you."* Isaiah 43:3

Chevy '59

Gen. Filemon Reodica Jr.

I miss the days when I would drive my '59 Chevy, and I would put my right arm over my wife's shoulders as we drove along. The design of the one-piece front seat made it possible for me and my wife to be close to each other. There was nothing between us. We were inseparable even in the car.

But later the children and the grandchildren, seated in the front seat, separated us. I miss those days too. But now, with the children and grandchildren no longer around, my wife and I are still separated in the front seat. Why? Because modern cars now have front seats with a control panel in the middle.

I miss my Chevy '59. ✺

A moment with the *Lord*
Lord, may nothing and no one ever separate me from your love. Amen.

A moment with the *Word*
"Who will separate us from the love of Christ?"   Romans 8:35

A confusing moment
(a story passed on to me by Anita Austria)

I was looking for my keys. They were not in my pockets. A quick search in the meeting room revealed nothing. Suddenly I realized that I must have left them in the car. Frantically, I headed for the parking lot. My wife has scolded me many times for leaving the keys in the ignition. My theory is that it is the best place to leave them. Her theory is the car will be stolen.

Her theory was right. The parking lot was empty. I immediately called the police. I gave them my location, confessed that I had left my keys in the car ignition, and that my car had been stolen. Then I made a frantic call to my wife.

"Honey," I stammered. (I always call her "honey" in times like these.) I narrated my situation and before I can finish, she hastened to say, "I dropped you off!"

Now it was time to be silent. Embarrassed, I said, "Well, come and get me." She retorted, "I will... as soon as I convince the policeman that I have not stolen your car!" ❈

A moment with the Lord
Lord, remind me that every problem has a reason, and has a solution.
Amen.

A moment with the Word
"Trust in the Lord, and do good... leave it to the Lord,
and wait patiently for Him."   Psalm 37:3-7

Forgetful

The story is told about an elderly husband who told his wife: "Get me ice cream from the refrigerator please." And he warned her not to be forgetful. The wife came back and brought him a hot dog instead, upon which the husband said: "See, I told you. You are really forgetful already! You forgot the catsup!" ✳

A moment with the 𝒮ord
Lord, help me not to forget that other people have faults,
and so do I. Amen.

A moment with the 𝒲ord
"God resists the proud but bestows His favor on the lowly." James 4:6

A heartwarming moment

Emily Cuaso

*I*t's more fun to be a senior citizen! My husband, Edwin, and I have a lot of funny moments as we journey together in the twilight of our years. We enjoy each other's company.

As senior citizens, we enjoy a 20% discount from restaurants, movies, grocery stores, etc. We understand what it means to have meaningful and quality time. As the saying goes, "Growing old is compulsory. Growing up is optional." We chose to grow old gracefully, with lots of acquired wisdom given to us by God.

We have been married for 37 years, have weathered many storms in life, and being together up to now is such a blessing from the Lord.

Being forgetful, losing things, being *makulit* is such an ordinary thing for us. As they say, it really comes with age. But, being deaf or pretending to be is another thing. One day, the doorbell rang and Edwin went out to check. There was a lady who was looking for me. So Edwin asked her name.

"*Sino yan?*" She said "*Si Babylyn po.*"

Edwin asked her again, "*Ano bibilhin?*"

Then she repeated, "*Si Babylyn po. Hinahanap ko po si Mam.*"

Edwin: "*Ano bibilhin ni Mam?*" Then he called me.

When I found out what happened, both of us started to laugh and enjoyed the moment. Every time I remember this incident, it makes me smile. ✺

A moment with the *Lord*
Lord, help me to live well, love much and laugh often. Amen.

A moment with the *Word*
"Be glad in the Lord, and rejoice, O righteous, and shout for joy, all you upright in heart." Psalm 32:11

Childlike humility

*I*t is always a pleasure to have 83-year-old Pete Santiago, a retired judge, in our pilgrimages. His wit and wisdom are awesome and inspiring. When he talks, all of us in the group, young or old, listen well so as not to miss a punchline, or a word of wisdom. But what I admire most in him is his ability to be humble and to really listen.

On our bus ride from Medjugorje to the Sarajevo airport, he went to the front, took the microphone, thanked everyone sincerely, and apologized to anyone he may have hurt, without meaning to, in thought, word, or deed.

That for me, is greatness — the ability of an elderly and successful person to be modest and humble like a child. ✸

A moment with the Lord
Lord, remind me that true greatness is in humility. Amen.

A moment with the Word
"Whoever makes himself great will be humbled, and whoever humbles himself will be made great." Matthew 23:12

Lost and found!

Nenne R. Bartolome

$\mathcal{I}$ went to a gift shop in San Francisco, California and bought a few things which I put in a shopping bag. I took a break and went to the huge comfort room. I hung my handbag which contained all my valuables, passport, monies, etc. on the back of the door and put my shopping bag on the floor. When I was done, I left hurriedly. As I was about to exit from the building, I realized I was carrying only the shopping bag! I froze and panicked. My heart beat so fast as I rushed with giant steps towards the CR. There were so many 'what ifs' on my mind, and I worried about what I would do if I lost that handbag which contained my 'life.' I went inside the cubicle, and there it was, exactly where I left it!

What a miracle! I never really thought I would still find my handbag in this city. But prayers really work. In my anxiety, I was uttering, "God, God, help me!"

I must say God has always been with me. Jesus, I trust in You! Mama Mary, I love you! ✺

A moment with the $\mathcal{L}$ord
Lord, increase my faith! Increase my trust in You. Amen.

A moment with the $\mathcal{W}$ord

"If you had faith like a mustard seed, you would say to this mulberry tree, 'Be uprooted and be planted in the sea; and it would obey you!'"

Luke 17:6

The little store

There is a little out-of-the way store selling simple souvenirs near Lake Galilee where many pilgrims' buses make a stop. It is owned by 77-year-old Abu Sarim who was expelled from a nearby pilgrimage site because he could not pay the rent. This kind and generous old man was like a father to many, if not to all the bus drivers. Out of gratitude to him, and to help him, they bring pilgrims to his little store.

Yes, we believe in the goodness of people. We believe that love begets love. And we believe that every person is worth stopping for. ✺

A moment with the *Lord*
Lord, remind me that every person is worth stopping for. Amen

A moment with the *Word*
"You must be compassionate, just as your Father is compassionate."
Luke 6:36

Lost luggage

Ambassador Mercy Tuason

*M*y sister, Betty, and I were in Rome to attend the beatification of Mother Teresa of Calcutta, and we were being given the chance to kiss Pope John Paul II's hand!

The taxi driver brought down Betty's luggage, and off he went his merry way with all my material possessions! Initially, I was in shock. How could I have forgotten my luggage! Now, what am I going to wear for the beatification? To kiss the Pope's hand, surely, one had to be decently dressed. Black formal wear and a veil would have been perfect.

Feelings of hesitation to buy clothes were further reinforced by a gentle pat from Mother Teresa who once said, "I will be a saint means I will despoil of myself of all that is not God; I will strip my heart of all created things; I will live in poverty and detachment; I will renounce my will, my inclinations, my whims and fancies and make myself a willing slave to the will of God."

At that moment, I thought: "Yes, Mother Teresa, I understand, one must be poor in spirit, too, but surely not poor, as in, no clothes to wear for a big day! As providence would have it, Betty and I are of the same size, and so off I went to kiss the Pope's hand in Betty's clothes, in Trining's veil, and the same black shoes I wore when I arrived.

Wasn't that quick and easy? And a perfect way to justify a senior moment! ❋

A moment with the *Lord*
*Lord, remind me that I do not need, and I can do
without a lot of things in this life. Amen.*

A moment with the *Word*
*"Your true life is not made up of things that you own,
no matter how rich you are."*   Luke 12:15

A Pilgrim's Prayer
John M. Haffert

*I*f some things do not happen as they are scheduled, Lord, may I remember that I am a pilgrim, not a tourist!

If I should get tired and inclined to become short-tempered, Lord, may I remember that I am a pilgrim, not a tourist!

If my meal in a foreign country may not be to my particular liking, Lord, may I remember that I am a pilgrim, not a tourist!

If any delays should occur and I should become anxious, Lord, may I remember that I am a pilgrim, not a tourist!

If some other pilgrim is making noise so that I cannot hear the guide, Lord, may I remember that I am a pilgrim, not a tourist, when I ask that person to be a bit quiet!

If someone takes a better seat or choice place, Lord, may I remember that I am a pilgrim, not a tourist! If I find myself last in line waiting, Lord, may I remember that I am a pilgrim, not a tourist!

If I should get a chance to help another person who always seems to be annoying me, Lord, may I remember that I am a pilgrim, not a tourist!

But Lord, especially let me remember that what I find objectionable in another is really what you oftentimes find objectionable in me, and let me remember this and forgive the other, as You are continually forgiving me! ✳

A moment with the *Lord*
Lord, remind me that I am a pilgrim, not a tourist in this life. Amen.

A moment with the *Word*
"Be kind and tender-hearted to one another, and forgive one another, as God has forgiven you through Christ." Ephesians 4:32

'Senior moment'- proof

Maria Lourdes Lopa

*M*y Papa has repeatedly shown us how amazing the effect of his devotion to Mama Mary is. Well, apart from all the blessings he has received through the intercession of Mama Mary, he has also proven that the Holy Rosary is "senior moment"-proof.

On several occasions, when it would have been quite impossible for my Papa to recite the entire Rosary, he surprises us by doing so. Papa had an operation in 1996 for subdural hematoma. He would go in and out of lucid moments then, but when it was time to pray the Rosary, he would be fully alert, lucid, and responsive.

When he had a mild stroke in 2007 he was totally disoriented, calling things by different names. And yet, he invited my Mom to pray the Rosary, and he was able to pray with her!

On the day my Papa passed away, he was already totally unresponsive. But when we all huddled around him to pray the Rosary, he responded with his eyes, a slight movement of his lips, and a gentle clasp of his hands! On one instance, when my sister who was leading the Rosary made a mistake with one of the mysteries, my Papa gripped her hand and made a facial expression to correct her!

What an amazing relationship my Papa had with Jesus and Mama Mary that during his most helpless moments, Mama Mary showed him that she was right there beside him. ✳

A moment with the *Lord*
Lord, help me not to doubt, belittle, or take for granted the Blessed Mother's love. Amen.

A moment with the *Word*
"Hail Mary, full of grace, the Lord is with you..."　　Luke 1:28

'Do I know you?'

Perla Michael

Last 2010 we had a family reunion and it was held in Bohol. One of the activities was a tour around the province. My 81-year-old sister, Nestora, and my 78-year-old brother, Joe, were seated together in the tourist bus. They chatted, and after almost an hour, my sister introduced herself to my brother, and then asked him: "Do I know you?"

He replied: "Are you crazy? I'm your brother, Joe!"

We could not help but laugh. But somehow, we also felt sad because my sister doesn't remember a lot of things now. So near, yet so distant. ✸

A moment with the Lord

Lord, thank You for the assurance that You will never forget me or be far from me. Amen.

A moment with the Word

"I have called you by name; You are mine."   Isaiah 43:1

Duty of delight

Geri Maiatico

*J*anuary 2011, I received word that my brother, Charles, was approaching his final days here on earth. Knowing that I would not be able to arrive in time from the Philippines to be with him, I called his 89-year-old godmother, Alice, who lived in the same town, and asked for prayers

Upon receiving my call, Alice immediately de-iced her car and drove several miles to be with my brother, her godson. She found him beautifully prepared by his hospice nurse to be received by our Lord. While he was not responsive, she took his hand, told him stories, and prayed with him until he quietly passed away.

Later I asked her why she had put herself at risk, driving alone in the middle of a cold winter night. She simply said, "It was my duty." I was his godmother, and I remember when I held this nine-pound baby in my arms during his christening in 1943. I have loved him all these 68 years, never stopped trying to be "present" to him. It was my duty, what I wanted and felt I was called upon to do."

It was, as the Catholic social activist, Dorothy Day, called a "duty of delight." How fortunate my brother had been to have this simple, unassuming woman by his side. How fortunate I felt to have her "present" to him when I could not be.

This incident prompted me to examine my own shortcomings as a godmother to several Filipino and American-born children. It prompted me to think about my own Christian commitment and what I might do, despite time and distance, to be more of a "presence" in their lives, beyond the typical Christmas and birthday remembrances. 🌸

A moment with the *L*ord
Lord, remind me that more than my presents,
it is my presence that really matters. Amen.

A moment with the *W*ord
"How precious is your lovingkindness O God!"   Psalm 36:7

Memories of our Lolo
Jarius Bondoc

*L*olo Elias wasn't our real *Lolo*. He was *Lola's* childhood beau who married our *Lola* after she was widowed.

Visits to *Lolo* Elias were memorable. He would give us a hug and a kiss, rub our shoulders with his prickly stubble, and would smell each one. He'd do that even when we were in our teens. I loved it whenever he whispered to me that I was his favorite grandchild, and so would smell me the longest.

One summer, six of us brothers and cousins spent the rowdiest school break with *Lola* and *Lolo*. After climbing trees and fishing the whole day, *Lolo* would hustle us to the shower to prepare us for piano lessons under *Lola*. He'd cook supper, pray the Rosary with us, then smell and tuck each of us into bed.

We lost *Lola* five days before Christmas of '66. A truck bumped a jitney that hit my *Lola* who was strolling. The five children and 19 grandchildren were inconsolable. We took turns sleeping in with *Lolo* Elias. Every night we heard sobbing. We would go to *Lolo's* bedroom. On the big bed would be spread out *Lola's* favorite dresses. *Lolo* would smell each dress, and cry himself to sleep.

A stroke paralyzed *Lolo* Elias in his sixties. We visited him at the hospital and later his retirement cabin. Lying in bed, he would ask me to lay my head on his chest so he could smell me. He would sob and whisper over and over that I was his favorite grandchild, and was so sorry he never bought me that big motorbike (which I never really wanted). When he passed away, his grandsons wept unashamedly.

Fr. Jerry M. Orbos, SVD

During family gatherings, we would share fond memories of *Lolo* Elias and wonder from what magical well *Lolo* Elias drew love. We felt so blessed to have been raised by such a loving *Lolo*.

In one such gathering, I recounted how *Lolo* Elias always had whispered to me that I was his pet grandchild. Tears welled in the eyes of my siblings and cousins. It wasn't because my revelation made them jealous. It was because *Lolo* Elias had whispered to each of them too that he/she was his favorite grandchild. *Lolo* Elias made each one of us feel special. ✺

A moment with the *Lord*
Lord, thank You for people who make us feel Your real and concrete love. Amen.

A moment with the *Word*
"Grandchildren are the crown of old men. And the glory of sons is their fathers."   Proverbs 17:6

'Apo, where are my slippers?'

Aida L. Velarde

J woke up early that bright Friday morning. I had to take *Lola* (grandmother) to the Black Nazarene in Quiapo, Manila. As we boarded a Quiapo-bound jeepney, I lovingly looked with admiration at *Lola* who was in her maroon dress and her favorite beaded, colorful slippers.

As we reached our destination, I wondered what was keeping *Lola* from getting off the jeepney. I heard her mutter something. Suddenly, to the amusement of our fellow passengers, *Lola* exclaimed, "*Apo*, where are my slippers?" Staring with knitted brows at *Lola's* curling toes, it dawned on me that *Lola* had taken off her beaded slippers when she boarded the jeepney! ✾

A moment with the *Lord*
*Lord, I believe that You will never leave me behind
nor forget me. Amen.*

A moment with the *Word*
*"Do not cast me off in the time of old age. Do not forsake me
when my strength fails."*   Psalm 71:9

The gift of friends
Belen Asuelo

My *Tatay* who lived all his life in the province had so many friends to keep. There was not a day that he wouldn't join them in small talks. At 82 years old, it was his habit to go out of the house early morning and late afternoon, just to talk to his fellow senior comrades at the "*kanto*."

When my brother and I brought him to Manila because of his failing health, we had to face the inevitable. He was confined in a hospital because of kidney failure. One early morning, he awoke with a smile on his face. The reason for the smile? With gladness, he told me that his friends visited him at the hospital a few minutes ago. I was the one who was with him the night before and there was no one who dropped by. It was also impossible for his friends from Samar to come over without me knowing it. When I asked him why I didn't see them, he replied that they were in a hurry to go because it was raining. Yes, indeed, rains were pouring outside. So I did not contradict him any further, for the joy of that visit was evident on my father's face.

My *Tatay* is now at peace with his other fellow departed friends. Looking back, I couldn't help but thank God for the gift of friendship. Life on earth bursts with happiness because of friends who journey with us. They give us a reason to smile and carry on. Thank You, Lord, for I am blessed with friends. ✵

A moment with the Lord
Lord, thank You for the gift of true, sincere,
lasting friends. Amen.

A moment with the Word
"Love one another with mutual affection; anticipate one
another in showing honor." I Corinthians 13:7

'Apostolate'

*D*id you hear the story about two long lost friends who met each other again after 40 years?

When asked about their work and present concerns, one of them said: "I am busy with my 'apostolate' — taking care of my *apos*." (grandchildren)

The other one said: "Media *ako. May* diabetes!"
(I have diabetes!)

Let us not forget to communicate joy, humor, hope and inspiration. That's why it is called good news! Especially in our sunset years! ✹

A moment with the *Lord*
*Lord, I may lose my memory, but help me not to lose
my sense of humor and trust in You. Amen.*

A moment with the *Word*
"Always be full of joy in the Lord. I say it again, rejoice."
Philippians 4:4

Stages of life
Lalin P. Basilio

*N*ormally when one reaches the age of forty, you would, in one way or the other, need reading glasses. At the age of fifty, you would be careful of your food intake and watchful of your weight. When you become sixty, you would concentrate more on your lifestyle, health and spiritual priorities.

At seventy, you slow down on your commitments and activities. And when one reaches the age of eighty, one is fully prepared and ready to face all circumstances in life. One is fulfilled, peaceful, happy and ready to journey towards a "new" life -- a life that is eternal and hopeful and free. ✺

A moment with the Lord
Lord, thank You for Your love and Your divine will. Amen.

A moment with the Word
"And surely I am with you always, to the very end of age."
Matthew 28:20

'Hu u?'
Adonis

On the occasion of my mom's 90th birthday, I said in my short speech for her:

"When I was still a baby, you left me with your sister's family so you could pursue post graduate studies in Medicine in the U.S. When you returned to the Philippines after four years, I couldn't recognize you and you became sad. I had grown up and made a living abroad for many years. Now I am here, and you couldn't recognize me anymore. It's my turn to be sad."

Alzheimer's disease just made my mom respond with a smile. And the audience smiled with her. ✳

A moment with the *Lord*
Lord, remind me that time spent together is precious and irreplaceable. Amen.

A moment with the *Word*
"How good and delightful to see kindred living together in unity."
Psalm 133:1

Five common regrets in life

Bronnie Ware

1. *I* wish I'd had the courage to live a life true to myself, not the life others expected of me.

   Most people have not honored even a half of their dreams and had to die knowing that it was due to choices they had made, or not made.

2. I wish I didn't work so hard.

   By simplifying your lifestyle and making conscious choices along the way, it is possible to not need the income that you think you do.

3. I wish I'd had the courage to express my feelings.

   Many people suppressed their feelings in order to keep peace with others. As a result, they settled for a mediocre existence and never became who they were truly capable of becoming.

4. I wish I had stayed in touch with my friends.

   It is common for anyone in a busy lifestyle to let friendships slip. But when you are faced with your approaching death, the physical details of life fall away. It is not money or status that holds the true importance for them. It all comes down to love and relationships in the end.

5. I wish that I had let myself be happier.

   Many did not realize until the end that happiness is a choice. They had stayed stuck in old patterns and habits. ✳

A moment with the Lord

Lord, may I have little or no regrets when I reach my sunset years.
Amen.

A moment with the Word

"A man's heart plans his way, but the Lord directs his steps."
Proverbs 16:9

Ready and free

"Prayer for a Happy Death"
by *President Corazon C. Aquino*

lmighty God, most merciful Father, You alone know the time. You alone know the hour. You alone know the moment when I shall breathe my last. So remind me each day, most loving Father, to be the best that I can be. To be humble, to be kind, to be patient, to be true; to embrace what is good, to reject what is evil, to adore only You.

When the final moment does come, let not my loved ones grieve for long. Let them comfort each other, and let them know how much happiness they brought into my life. Let them pray for me, as I will continue to pray for them, hoping that they will always pray for each other.

Let them know that they made possible whatever good I offered to our world. And let them realize that our separation is just for a short while as we prepare for our reunion in eternity.

Our Father in heaven, You alone are my hope, You alone are my salvation. Thank You for Your unconditional love. Amen. ✳

A moment with the Lord
*Lord, grant me the grace of a meaningful life
and a happy death. Amen.*

A moment with the Word
*"I have fought the good fight, I have finished the race,
I have kept the faith."*　　2 Timothy 4:7-8

Bedtime prayer

Galoy Marfil

"*And now I lay me down to sleep*
I pray the Lord my soul to keep
And if I die before I wake
I pray the Lord my soul to take.
Amen."

I learned this poem from my mom when I was a child. Up to now, I whisper it consciously or subconsciously, at the end of each day before retiring to bed. It sounds sad, but trusting. Every time I say it, I add some words of praise and thanksgiving.

When my Mom reached her senior years, her once lucid memory was impaired. She could no longer recognize us in the family. Her condition worsened after her operation for a partial hip replacement due to a traumatic fall. She became anxious. She could no longer express her thoughts.

One evening, before putting her to bed, I recited and prayed this poem with her. She nodded and listened intently. With excitement, she said repeatedly, "I like that. I like that!"

We both smiled. ☀

A moment with the Lord
Lord, thank You for people who gave us lessons
and examples, for life! Amen.

A moment with the Word
"*The Lord bless you and keep you; the Lord make His face to shine*
upon you and be gracious to you…" Numbers 6:24-26

All for love

Ria Salgado Llanes

My mother, Cielo Macapagal Salgado, was heartbroken when my family and I migrated to Canada in 2001, and my sister, Cris, and her family followed six months later. However, she made it a point to visit us often. On one of her trips, her flight from Manila was delayed, and she arrived at her point of entry much later than expected. She still had to pass through immigration and customs, and check in at the airline counter for her connecting flight.

Mom brought a big bag of *tuyo* for Cris which she painstakingly sealed in plastic wrap and placed in her handcarry luggage. The bag was over the weight limit but Mom opted to pay a fee instead of leaving the *tuyo* behind. She certainly didn't want to disappoint Cris. After checking in, Mom only had a few minutes to reach the gate since the passengers were already boarding. She had to make a run for it. Mom was 64 at that time and it was certainly no mean feat to run across the Vancouver airport, even for someone much younger than she was. But she was able to catch her flight.

Later, Mom thanked me for giving her the comfortable shoes she was wearing when she did her "amazing race." I believe it was not those shoes, but her love for us, that helped her accomplish such a feat. ✳

A moment with the $\mathcal{L}$ord
Lord, thank You for our mothers who love us and who go out of their way for us. Amen.

A moment with the $\mathcal{W}$ord
"Can a woman forget her own baby and not love the child she bore? Even if a mother should forget her child, I will never forget you."
Isaiah 49:15

Why not?

Girlie

$\mathcal{I}$ t was my aunt's 90th grand birthday celebration in a posh restaurant. Close friends and relatives honored a much-loved matriarch. It was a happy feast. There were surprise numbers from her grandchildren and short speeches from family members. As everyone was enjoying the program, the toastmaster asked the audience: "So who wants to reach the age of 90 like Mommy?" The lively chatter stopped and there was silence for a few seconds, until a hand was raised, and this person was applauded.

I was in my early 40s then. Why did I not want to reach 90? What stopped me and the others? Fear of the future? Will I be able to sustain myself? Will I receive the same love and care?

Forgive me, Lord, for the many times I feared and doubted. ✴

A moment with the *Lord*

Lord, help me to see that growing old is a privilege and a blessing, and not a burden or a sad ending. Amen.

A moment with the *Word*

"The Lord is my shepherd; I have everything I need; He lets me rest in green meadows; he leads me beside peaceful streams…" Psalm 23

Missing a daughter

George Cuadra

We can never know or imagine how much a mother can love and sacrifice for her children.

My good friend decided to go to America some years back in search of a better future, leaving her 80- year-old mother behind. It was painful for her mother to let go of her but let go she did, because of love.

Now her mother is ill and alone, and she cannot be beside her. She wants to come home to take care of her, but her immigration papers in America are not in order.

One time she advised me: "No matter what happens, don't leave your own Papa behind. Never mind if you don't have much in life. As long as you are together, you will get by."

She misses her beloved daughter so much, and it breaks my heart to see her cry. She made me promise not to tell her daughter how much she missed her, especially at night, when there was no one by her side. ✳

A moment with the Lord
Lord, may I have no regrets when it comes to loving. Amen.

A moment with the Word
"Honor your father and your mother, as the Lord your God has commanded you."   Deuteronomy 5:16

A heart's memory

Doris Dizon

Christmas 2007.

Everyone was going to be home for Christmas. For the first time after many years, Mom, her children, grandchildren and great grandchildren will be together. This will be a wonderful Christmas!

Mom was 88 years old, and she has had Alzheimer's disease for some time. She remembered the names of her children and grandchildren, but not the face that went with each name. Conversations with Mom were mostly one-sided, with simple questions that, at times, were not answered. She was mostly silent, but always had a welcoming smile. She was still so carefully conscious of what she ate, and comfortable only with her "nanny" for her personal needs.

I looked at her, and I felt apprehensive. This wasn't my Mom! I did not know how to be with her. I was sad, watching her and not seeing the Mom I knew.

It's Christmas Eve — midnight Mass, *noche buena*, gift giving. There must be photos for posterity — photos of Mom with her children, with grandchildren and great grandchildren.

It was then my turn to have my photo taken with Mom. I felt her hold on my arms— tight, steady and comforting. Just like the way it used to be. It was then that I knew. Alzheimer's disease may have affected her mind, but never her heart.

So, yes, I will always believe. A heart keeps the moments that matter. The heart will not forget. ✳

A moment with the Lord
Lord, thank You that even when the mind fails,
the memory of the heart remains. Amen.

A moment with the Word
"You were mine. Before I formed you, I knew you.
And before you were born, I consecrated you."   Jeremiah 1:5

Psalm 23 for Senior Citizens

*S*haring with you the Psalm 23 version for senior citizens:

"Though I walk through the valley of Senior Moments, I shall fear no panic, for my senior discount card is with me. A pair of reading glasses in each room shall comfort me. Surely a receding hairline shall follow me all the days of my life. And I shall dwell in the restaurants of The Early Bird Special and enjoy my retirement." ✸

A moment with the *Lord*

Lord, thank You for your countless blessings through the years, till the end. Amen.

A moment with the *Word*

"Even to your old age, I shall be the same; and even to your graying years I shall bear you; I have done it and I shall carry you…"   Isaiah 46:4

One little rose

Through the years, I have always emphasized the need, the urgency of expressing our love to our loved ones while they are still alive.

Here is a beautiful poem I read with a poignant but very important message.

One Little Rose

I would rather have one little rose
From the garden of a friend
Than to have the choicest flowers
When my stay on earth must end...

I would rather have one pleasant word
In kindness said to me
Than flattery when my heart is still
And life has ceased to be...

I would rather have a loving smile
From friends I know are true
Than tears shed 'round my casket
When this world I've bid adieu...

Bring me all your flowers today
Whether pink, or white, or red
I'd rather have one blossom now
Than a truckload when I'm dead.

A moment with the Lord

Lord, help me to love now.
Help me not to postpone my loving. Amen.

A moment with the Word

"Love never fails."   *I Corinthians 13:8*

When Irish eyes are smiling

Adele Joaquin

*M*y mother, afflicted with vascular dementia, tends to be repetitive. One morning, we had a friend, visiting from Ireland. Her name was Kathleen.

Nanay asked her, "What's that Irish song you usually sing?"

Kathleen replied: "When Irish Eyes are Smiling."

Nanay said, "Can you sing it for me?"

Kathleen gladly sings a few lines for *Nanay* and after a few seconds, *Nanay* again asked: "What's that Irish song you usually sing?"

Nanay must have asked the same question four times, and Kathleen obliged to sing the song for her. But on the fifth time Kathleen said, "I think we need a tape recorder here." Still she sang for *Nanay*, but when asked for the nth time what song the Irish usually sing, Kathleen said, "Danny Boy."

To our surprise, *Nanay* blurted out, "No. When Irish Eyes are Smiling!" ✹

A moment with the *Lord*
Lord, thank You for delightful moments spent with loved ones.
Amen.

A moment with the *Word*
"A merry heart does good, like medicine."
Proverbs 17:22

My humbling senior moment

Baby Almeda
(joined our Creator on June 18, 2013)

My doctor told me I have cancer in my right lung. At first, I couldn't believe it. I felt numb. I did not cry and I didn't show any resentment. I never questioned the Lord and I accepted my condition wholeheartedly. I smiled and humbly said, "If this is Your will my Lord, thank You!"

Some of my priest friends visited me – Fr. Jerry Orbos, Father Gerard, Father Mustaf, and also, dear Fatima Soriano. While Fatima prayed with me, she told me that the Blessed Mother was smiling and that she would take care of me!

I never doubted the Lord's presence and Mama Mary's steadfast love for me. While I was in the operating room, I continuously recited these lines: "Jesus, I trust in You. Mama Mary, I love you," until I fell asleep from the anesthesia.

This humbling moment that I experienced has strengthened my faith. I have offered all my sufferings and joys to Him. Thank You, Lord, my Master and my friend! ✸

A moment with the *Lord*

Lord, my Master and my friend, Thy will be done. Amen.

A moment with the *Word*

"Even when I walk through the dark valley of death, I will not be afraid for You are close beside me. Your rod and Your staff protect and comfort me." Psalm 23

Faces and phases

*T*he story is told about a group of girlfriends who regularly meet at the Ocean View restaurant for different reasons.

When they were in their teens, they agreed to meet there because the food was cheap, and there was this cute boy who lived on the same street. When they were in their twenties, they meet there because the beer was cheap, and the band was good.

When they advanced in years, they still agreed to meet there because it was right next to the gym where they can do workouts. The restaurant also served fish dishes which were good for their cholesterol count, and offered senior citizen discounts. More so, the staff was friendly to senior citizens, the handicapped, etc.

Through the years, the girlfriends kept in touch. One fine day, this group of now 85-year-olds discussed where to meet for dinner. After a lengthy discussion, they finally agreed to meet at the Ocean View restaurant.

Why? Because all of them said they had never dined there before! ✳

A moment with the *Lord*
Lord, thank You for the many faces, and phases in my life. Amen.

A moment with the *Word*
"With a long life I will satisfy him, and let him behold my salvation."
Proverbs 16:31

Getting stronger

*T*he story is told about an old woman who started the Stations of the Cross on the wrong end. The priest noticed this, approached her and said: "Grandma, I think you started on the 14th station where Jesus was laid in the tomb. You should have started on the 1st station where Jesus was condemned to die."

"Oh, no wonder I got the feeling that Jesus was getting stronger and stronger as I went from station to station," was her embarrassed reply. ✳

A moment with the *Lord*
Lord, help me to get stronger and become better as I move from station to station in life. Amen.

A moment with the *Word*
"Don't be afraid for I am with you. Don't be discouraged, for I am your God. I will strengthen you and help you."   Isaiah 41:10

Missing a turn

Fr. Dennis Flynn, SVD

Having been a missionary to the Philippines for many years, particularly in Mindoro, I have been familiar with the roads, with all their bumps, twists and turns, especially the cut-off points.

One time, on our way back to Calapan from a *Mangyan* Village in Mansalay, I realized that we were on an unfamiliar stretch of highway. How could I have missed the cut-off point? The very first thought to cross my now going on 79-year-old mind, was incipient Alzheimer's or at least, its consoling version, "a senior moment."

Later on, the most plausible explanation occurred to me. Traveling with me were three companions, with a nun seated on the passenger side. I wasn't so focused on my driving because I was trying so hard to use modest and acceptable vocabulary, and not my usual rough language among sailors and marines! And that made me miss the turn! ✳

A moment with the Lord
Lord, remind me that with all its twists and turns, life's road will lead to You in the end. Amen.

A moment with the Word
"Treasure my words in your heart; listen to my directions and you will live." Proverbs 4:4

On fire!
Malou Teano Estrada

*I*n one Easter Vigil Mass, we were asked by Fr. Jerry Orbos to light our candles during the renewal of baptismal vows. So focused on the ceremony, I closed my eyes in deep prayer. Then I smelled something burning! *Tito* Manny Magbag's *barong tagalog* was on fire! Thanks to *Tito* Manny's calmness, the fire was quickly put off, and we proceeded with the Mass with no commotion or interruption.

I would like to thank *Tito* Manny and *Tita* Lina for their kind understanding. In my senior years, I may become forgetful at times, but I never forget the kindness, understanding, and kind consideration of friends. ✻

A moment with the Lord
Lord, help me not to overlook other people's kindness, goodness, understanding, and love. Amen.

A moment with the Word
"Put on then, as God's chosen ones, compassionate hearts, kindness, humility, meekness and patience."   *Colossians 3:12*

Shortest caroling

Julie Munsayac

*E*very December in our community, we go caroling to earn funds for our various projects. The senior citizens just love us, and our singing.

It was around 9 o' clock in the evening when we were received by an elderly couple who were well into their 80s. We started with a little introduction and narration, followed by an opening song. When we were into our second song, the head of the elderly man started to bob, indicating that he was falling asleep. And soon after, his wife followed suit. But since we could not be rude, we continued and sang our third song. By the time we reached the chorus of our third song, our elderly audience was way into dreamland, with a few snores every now and then.

It was Father JB who made the decision to stop right there and then and let our sleepy audience get their much needed rest. Father JB called their caregiver who gently woke them up, and he announced that we had finished our rendition.

The couple smiled, stood up and asked their caregiver to lead us to the dining room for snacks.

That was the shortest caroling we ever had. ✺

A moment with the *Lord*
Lord, help me to remember that my plans should be tempered with other people's plans, and subject to Your plan. Amen.

A moment with the *Word*
"The heart of man disposeth his way; but the Lord must direct his steps." Proverbs 16:9

Bell or no bell
Pamela Navarro

This is a story about my late confessor, Fr. Andy Lussier. I remember one of his hilarious moments when he was saying Mass in the barrio.

A native boy told him that since there was no bell for the Consecration, he will just improvise one, so Father Andy said, "That is good. Thank you."

He thought he will just get an ice cream bell. During the Mass, when he raised the host, he was a little astonished when he heard a different sound.

The boy was shaking an old can of condensed milk filled with stones. After the celebration, he approached the boy with a smile and said, "That was really nice of you. But it is OK if we do not have a bell.

The following Sunday, another funny incident happened during the Consecration. When Father Andy raised the host, the boy suddenly said, "*Katakatak, katakatak, katakatak.*" Father Andy was shocked. He looked at the boy, nodding his head, motioning him to stop. But the boy did the same when he raised the chalice.

Father Andy said with a laugh: "This is an unforgettable experience!" ✳

A moment with the *Lord*
Lord, remind me that You will always provide. Amen.

A moment with the *Word*
"For God has not given us a spirit of timidity, but of power and love and discipline." 2 Timothy 1:7

The house dress
Lily Hubalde

*W*e arrived in Iloilo for our two-day JOLT (Journey to a Life in the Trinity) seminar.

We started unpacking our clothes, and since we lay speakers are all senior citizens, we rested for a while after unpacking. Sis. Susan Ilagan, 69 years old, got up and opened the closet, looking for something, then opened her suitcase and brought out the remaining contents. Not finding what she was looking for, she returned to the closet and searched. I asked her what she was looking for and, if she needed some help, but she didn't answer. She looked again in her suitcase for the third time. Then all of a sudden, she burst into a loud and uncontrollable laughter. And since we didn't know what was happening, we waited for her laughter to subside.

"Why?" I asked. She told us that she was looking for her house dress, and just as she was getting up for the fourth time to search in the closet, she realized that she was already wearing it! ✷

A moment with the *Lord*
Lord, remind me that what I am looking for in life are already in me and near me. Amen.

A moment with the *Word*
"Lord, to whom can we go? You have the words of eternal life."
John 6:68

Wireless

Ditas Lerma

I absolutely cannot live without my cell phone, so to make sure I don't leave it behind, I make it a point to return it to my handbag after each call or text message. One day, I got a call from a friend and, true to my habit, I put the phone in my bag once the call was over, then left the house to go to the mall.

About half an hour later, I heard my phone signaling that I have a text message. The message was from my eldest son, Francis, and it said: "Mom, you also brought with you the wireless!"

True enough, there, in my handbag with my wallet and other paraphernalia, was the wireless landline phone! ❋

A moment with the *Lord*
Lord, remind me that You will reach out to me
in any and every way You can. Amen.

A moment with the *Word*
"You know everything I do; from far away,
You understand all my thoughts."   Psalm 39:2

Someone's calling

Susan R. Grau

I enjoy being on the phone for hours, talking with friends. You can call me a "telefonista." One early evening, I was tinkering in the house when my husband, Ed, and my daughter, Katrina, who were in the bedroom, called me to say, "Someone's calling." I rushed to my bed, propped up my pillows, ready for a long haul. My eyeglasses were hanging from my neck. As I was about to make myself comfy, I put on my glasses slowly, and said, "Hello."

My husband and daughter stared at me, and let out guffaws of laughter. ✳

A moment with the *Lord*
Lord, help me to receive and answer Your call anytime, and in any way You so desire. Amen.

A moment with the *Word*
"Here am I, Lord; I come to do Your will."   Psalm 40:2

Professor emeritus
Dr. Carmelo A. Alfiler

*D*r. AC, a 72-year-old emeritus professor from a Philippine medical school, was about to finish his 8 a.m. - 9 a.m. lecture before 3rd year medical students when he got a call on his mobile phone from one of his residents in the nearby hospital, reminding him that the case conference he scheduled was about to start in 15 minutes. He assured the caller that he would make it as he only had to walk for five minutes from where he was.

One hour later, he got another call telling him that everyone in the conference room was already restless. "Thanks for the reminder," he graciously answered, "but I am now in my pajamas, ready for my afternoon nap."

A moment with the *Lord*
Lord, when the time comes that my intelligence would fade, let my thoughtfulness remain. Amen.

A moment with the *Word*
"Let not kindness and fidelity leave you."   Proverbs 3:3

Wrong side
Georgina Pia

*M*y best friend's dad, Dr. Mequi, in one of his formal meetings, noticed that everyone was staring at him. They had unusual smiles on their faces. Then his secretary said, "Sir, *baliktad po polo nyo.*"

He simply said, "I know, style *yan.*" He wore it that way, the whole day!

In another instance, in a mall, he thought that because he was a government official, people looked at him and smiled. When he saw himself on a mirror, lo and behold, there was no lens on one side of his eyeglasses!

He hardly noticed it, and gave us a good reason — "senior moments!" ✴

A moment with the ℒord
Lord, remind me that if there's a will, there's a way,
and there's a way out. Amen.

A moment with the 𝒲ord
"For I know the plans I have for you... plans to prosper you...
to give you a future and a hope."   Jeremiah 29:11

Two old friends

The story is is told about two old men who saw each other in the elevator. They just kept looking at each other, trying to recall where they met. Finally, one of them said; "Hey, I know you, but I just can't remember... ah, was it you or was it your brother who died?!" ❁

A moment with the ℒord
Lord, I may forget names, but help me not to forget friends.
Amen.

A moment with the 𝒲ord
"You did not choose me. I chose you." John 15:16

'Look at my feet!'

Juris Umali Soliman

I was cleaning my toe nails, removing old nail polish with acetone when suddenly there was no electricity. I didn't bother to turn on the emergency light since it was almost midnight.

When I woke up at 5:30 a.m., there was a heavy downpour but electricity was back. My maid and I started to bring things up to the second floor. I was worried that this heavy downpour would cause the creek at the back of my house to overflow and flood my first floor. I decided to attend the 6:45 a.m. Mass. Then I prayed in the Adoration Chapel for two hours, without realizing it. When I got home, I removed my sandals. I was astonished to see that I was not able to remove the nail polish on my right foot! Oh, no! My left foot without nail polish, and my right foot with polish!

Ha!ha!ha! "Senior moments!" I didn't even notice this when I removed my sandals before entering the Adoration Chapel.

I'm glad Jesus doesn't look at one's feet but at one's heart! He knows how my heart bleeds sometimes. He knows how I cry because of my helplessness, seeing the suffering of poor people around me. At that moment, Jesus removed the pains in my heart. He made me laugh at myself. Thank you, Jesus!

Cheers, my dear sixty-zens! ✺

A moment with the Lord
Lord, help me to always see the good, the right,
and the beautiful in life. Amen.

A moment with the Word
"You are good, and do good; teach me Your statutes."
Psalm 119:68

Sunglasses on
Letty Syquia

One time I was tinkering with my mobile phone. Suddenly, I saw something move. I panicked, not quite knowing what to make out of it. After pressing some buttons, I found out that my mobile phone had a camera, and I had pressed the video function!

On another occasion, I arrived home from work, and the house was dark. I reprimanded our helper for not putting on the lights. Her simple reply was: "You are still wearing your sunglasses, Ma'am!" ☀

A moment with the *Lord*
Lord, help me to see the humor and the surprises
strewn all throughout my path. Amen.

A moment with the *Word*
"Teach me, O Lord, Your way, lead me along a straight path."
Psalm 27:1

Generation gap
(a story passed on to me)

A self-important college freshman, walking along the beach, took it upon himself to explain to a senior citizen resting on the chair, why it was impossible for the older generation to understand his generation.

"You grew up in a different world, actually an almost primitive one," the student said loud enough for others to hear. "The young people of today grew up with television, jet planes, space travel, and man walking on the moon. We have nuclear energy, ships and cell phones, computers with light speed... and many more." After a brief silence, the senior citizen responded: "You're right, son. We didn't have those things when we were young... so we invented them. Now, young man, what are you doing for the next generation?" ✺

A moment with the *Lord*
Lord, teach me to be humble, and to respect and appreciate those who have gone ahead of me. Amen.

A moment with the *Word*
"A gray head is a crown of glory; It is found in the way of righteousness."   *Proverbs 16:31*

Me, retire?

Elmer Sarmiento

$\mathcal{I}$ 'm turning 57 and I believe that I am still young. I run, log thousands of miles a month on business trips, work harder than ever, and from time to time, I play with my grandchildren. Yes, I now have two grandchildren who brighten my day and that of my wife's.

I don't know if I should look forward to the day that I will become a senior citizen. It seems I can't make up my mind as to how to approach this life event. I take each day as it comes.

A lot of people who know me tell me that I will not ever retire. Retire? Retire means you are tired twice! Perhaps they mean a career change – from a business executive to perhaps, a doting grandpa. That seems delightful!

I admire the late Jesse Robredo. He was a great man. He made a lot of difference in the lives of his family, and in the lives of ordinary people. He was a quiet presence. Taking inspiration from him, I will try to do the following as I journey to my senior years:

1. Say "I love you" always to my wife and children, and to my grandchildren.
2. Report to my wife daily and go home immediately after work.
3. Fix anything that needs fixing in the house.
4. Be more prayerful.

I can't be a Jesse Robredo. All I want is to be a great man to my wife and family. ✺

A moment with the ℒord
Lord, help me to make the rest of my life, the best of my life. Amen.

A moment with the 𝒲ord
"They will still yield fruit in old age; they shall be full of sap and very green."   Psalm 92:14

Gratitude

Gratitude is the best attitude especially in the sunset years of our lives.

If you can say "yes" and "thank you" for everything, and to everyone that has come into your life, then you are peaceful and free! Do not dwell on the could-have-beens and the should-have-beens.

If you stop asking why about anything or anyone in your present life, then you are free to move on.

If you stop being crippled by "what-ifs" or "maybes," then you can face tomorrow without fear.

When you say "thanks," you say goodbye to worries.

When you say "thanks," you say goodbye to problems.

When you say "thanks," you say goodbye to regrets. 🌸

A moment with the ℒord
Lord, thank You for everything and everyone in my life. Amen.

A moment with the 𝒲ord
"I will give thanks to the Lord with all my heart."   Psalm 9:1

🌸 84   Fr. Jerry M. Orbos, SVD

At the setting of the sun

It is not the thing that you do, dear
it's the thing you could have done
that leaves me with a bit of heartache
at the setting of the sun."

May we never hear a loved one say something like this to us, and be filled with regrets that we loved too little, too late at the setting of the sun.

Do not postpone your loving.

Do not postpone your giving.

Do not postpone your forgiving. ※

A moment with the *Lord*
Lord, help me to truly love right here and right now. Amen.

A moment with the *Word*
"I have loved you with an everlasting love, so I continue to show you my constant love." Jeremiah 31:3

At peace before God

Lord, sometimes when I cannot pray, I sit very still with nothing to say. Nevertheless I know You are there, and I whisper Your name, because I know You care. You know the troubles in my mind. You know my weaknesses and the failures in my life, and at times, my doubts, worries and fears. I know that Your spirit is with me, and that You will never leave me nor abandon me, ever. And so in the silence of my heart, I will listen only to Your sweet voice, hear Your tender but true words, and feel Your embrace. In You alone will I trust, put my faith, and surrender everything. Amen."

A moment with the Lord
Lord, thank You for being with me, always. Amen.

A moment with the Word
"Be still and know that I am God."   Psalm 46:10

Beatitudes for friends of the aged

Blessed are they who understand my faltering steps and shaking hand.

Blessed are they who know that my ears today must strain to catch the words they say.

Blessed are they who seem to know that my eyes are dim and my wits are slow.

Blessed are they who looked away when my coffee spilled today.

Blessed are they who, with a cheery smile, stopped to chat for a while.

Blessed are they who never say, "You've told that story twice today."

Blessed are they who know the ways to bring back lovely yesterdays.

Blessed are they who make it known that I am loved, not left alone.

Blessed are they who know the loss of strength which I need to bear the cross.

Blessed are they who ease the days on my journey home in so many loving ways." ✳

A moment with the Lord
Lord, thank You for people who care, who help, who understand me, whoever I am, in spite of who I am. Amen.

A moment with the Word
"If we love one another, God dwells in us, and His love is brought to perfection in us." 1 John 4:12

Prayer When Growing Older

(taken from Straight from the Heart prayer companion)

*D*ear Lord, I may be growing older,
But I'll never outgrow my need to talk with You.
I've come a long way in my life.
And I thank You for helping me to get this far.
May You continue to watch over me each day.

You are my dearest Friend,
and You know I've had my ups and downs in life.
Although there have been some sorrows,
I've also been blessed with many joys.
Now that I'm in my later years,
please give me the strength and energy
to carry on in the best ways I can.
I'm so glad to be alive, Lord.
Keep me safe from harm.

Let me be as free as possible from any health
problems and financial worries.
I hope to take things a little easier at this time in my life.
Of course at my age, I'm not able to do
quite as much as I used to.
I'm slower now and sometimes it takes me a while to get going.
So please help others to be kind, patient, and
understanding toward me.
And may I always remember to treat them the same way.

Lord, let me look forward to each new day.
Be merciful and bless my remaining years with happiness
and loved ones who care.
In Jesus' name. Amen."

pg. 246

United and reunited

*M*y greatest joy is that we as a family are united in this life, and my greatest wish is that we will all be reunited in heaven someday."

Since we were little children, and up to now, this has been Mama's constant reminder to us.

"My greatest sorrow is if anyone of you in our family would not make it to heaven."

Simple words.
Powerful words.
Inspiring words. ❋

A moment with the *Lord*
*Lord, help us to do Your will now so that we will be
reunited in heaven forever. Amen.*

A moment with the *Word*
"Set your heart on the things that are in heaven."
Colossians 3:1-2

Autumn

Of the four seasons, I like autumn best. Maybe it's because of the vibrant and awesome colors of autumn, or the melancholy of the season.

Autumn is the time when one who has endured the noonday sun, can rest, look back, just be, and say to oneself, "What is done is done. I did the best I can."

In the autumn of our lives, may we be filled, not with regrets, but with serenity, peace and happiness. ✳

A moment with the *Lord*
Lord, in all the seasons of my life, please stay with me and be my light. Amen.

A moment with the *Word*
"Come, I will lead you into solitude, and there, I will speak tenderly to your heart. I will be true and faithful." Hosea 2:19-20

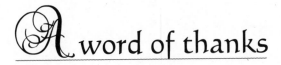

A word of thanks

My sincerest thanks to the
"Moments with Fr. Jerry Foundation" members
who have helped me generously
in my media apostolate:
Ella Sanchez, Nenne Bartolome, Nita Trofeo, Malou Estrada
Bayani & Anita Ting, Lalin Basilio, Fritzie Lopez,
Nemy Platon, Rebbie Garcia, Lilibeth Francisco,
Lydia Tagle, Juris Soliman, Vivian Eleazar, Manny Magbag
Sylvia Pascual, Flor Bello, Maita Martinez,
Adrian Panganiban, Grace Tan, and Celi Sarabia.

My heartfelt thanks also to
Angie Gabriel for compiling the selections
Amy Abitria and Marie Susannie Carlit
for typing the manuscripts,
Alexis Dizon for the cover photograph,
Galoy Marfil for cover design and layout;
Oscar & Mila Balaoing for supporting me in this project.

Thank you, dear friends!
Whether junior or senior,
may we have many memorable moments!

SVD Mission Office, P.O. Box 1375, Manila, Philippines
Tel. (632) 721-7457; (632) 4147044 Telefax (632) 727-1160
E-mail: jmo1053@gmail.com

God bless you.
Mama Mary loves you!